The Urbana Free Library

To renew materials call
217-367-4057

BIG IDEAS in SCIENCE

GENETICS

Lynette Brent Sandvold

11/09

This edition first published in 2010 in the United States
of America by Marshall Cavendish Benchmark.

Marshall Cavendish Benchmark
99 White Plains Road
Tarrytown, NY 10591
www.marshallcavendish.us

Library of Congress Cataloging-in-Publication Data
Sandvold, Lynette Brent.
Genetics / by Lynette Brent Sandvold.
p. cm. — (Big ideas in science)
Summary: "Provides comprehensive information on the theory of genetics
and how it affects our lives today"—Provided by publisher.
Includes bibliographical references and index.
ISBN 978-0-7614-4396-4
1. Genetics—Juvenile literature. 2. DNA—Juvenile literature.
3. Genes—Juvenile literature. I. Title.
QH437.5.S26 2010
576.5—dc22
2008055990

The photographs in this book are used by permission and through the courtesy of:
Cover: Q2AMedia Art Bank
Half Title: Henk Bentlage/Shutterstock.
P4: Tom & Dee Ann McCarthy/Corbis; P5br: Photolibrary; P5t: BigStockPhoto; P7: Dennis Macdonald/Photolibrary;
P8ctl: Lev Dolgachov/Shutterstock; P7ctr: Shutterstock; P8cl: Dreamstime; P8cr: Shutterstock; P8cbl: Q2AMedia Picture Bank;
P8cbr: Q2AMedia Picture Bank; P8bl: Shutterstock; P8br: Shutterstock; P9: Shutterstock; P10: Shutterstock;
P12: Bettmann/Corbis; P13: Thomas/Shutterstock; P14: Bettman/Corbis; P15: Dreamstime; P16-17: Photolibrary;
P16: Interfoto Pressebildagentur/Alamy; P18: Bettmann/Corbis; P19t: Dreamstime; P19b: Fotolia; P20-21: Paula Cobleigh/
Shutterstock; P22: Dreamstime; P23: Barbara McClintock; P24: Photolibrary; P26: Photolibrary; P27bg: Fotolia; P27: Phototake
Inc./Alamy; P28: Oregon State University; P30: Dreamstime; P31: Fotolia; P32: Spencer Grant/Photolibrary; P34: Charles
Dharapak/Associated Press; P35tr: Shutterstock; P35b: Shutterstock; P36: Fotolia; P38-39: Index Stock Imagery/Photolibrary;
P39: Sandra Cunningham/Shutterstock; P40 Box: Shutterstock; Shutterstock; Shutterstock; Shutterstock; Shutterstock;
Shutterstock; P41: Shutterstock; P43t: Q2AMedia Picture Bank; P43b: Shutterstock; P44: Photolibrary; P45: Ho Old/Reuters.
Illustrations: Q2AMedia Art Bank

Created by Q2AMedia
Art Director: Sumit Charles
Editor: Denise Pangia
Series Editor: Penny Dowdy
Client Service Manager: Santosh Vasudevan
Project Manager: Shekhar Kapur
Designer: Shilpi Sarkar
Illustrators: Prachand Verma, Ajay Sharma,
Bibin Jose, Abhideep Jha and Rajesh Das
Photo Research: Shreya Sharma

Printed in Malaysia

135642

Contents

What Is Genetics?

"You get your height from your dad's side of the family." "Look! She has her mother's eyes." Have you ever heard anyone say something like this? If you have, then you already know a little about the science called genetics.

Picture a family portrait. The son is tall, the uncle is tall, and the grandfather is tall. The family's height may be the result of heredity, which is the passing on of characteristics from one generation to the next. Because of heredity, family members often look like one another. Heredity ensures that dogs give birth to puppies instead of kittens. Heredity occurs not only in humans and animals, but in other living things as well. Plants, bacteria, and even fungi are subject to heredity. The study of heredity is called genetics, and the scientists who study genetics are called geneticists.

In this family, as in all families, traits have been passed on from one generation to the next.

Why might you be left-handed just like your mom? You get your traits from your ancestors. A trait is a characteristic like eye color, the shape of your nose, or being right- or left-handed. Traits start inside of cells. Your entire body is made of cells. Cells are so small they can only be seen under a microscope. Inside each of the cells are structures that are even tinier. One of the structures is called a **gene**, which carries those traits like eye color and height from one generation to the next. Builders need plans to build houses. Just like house plans, genes are the plans to build living things.

You may not know it, but genetics are a big part of the world around you. Detectives use genetic science to solve crimes. Doctors use genetics to make people healthier. Scientists use genetics to make food better. The science of genetics is new. We've only begun to scratch the surface of genetics in the last fifty years or so. Yet, the idea of heredity has been around for a long time. Genetics has a fascinating history. It can also make us stronger, healthier, and safer.

Since cells are so small, they can only be seen under a microscope.

Scientists are working toward creating a tomato that contains a full day's serving of the nutrient folate.

DNA and Chromosomes

The Basics

Even if you have your dad's height and your mom's eyes, you are still unique. DNA and chromosomes make each of us different. But how do they work?

DNA is short for deoxyribonucleic acid. Where do you find DNA? In cells! Cells are the smallest parts of every living thing, from mushrooms to pine trees to whales. Those tiny cells have even smaller parts. One part is a membrane. A membrane is like a wall around the cell that keeps the insides safe. The membrane does allow some things, like sugars, to pass in and out of the cell wall. The cytoplasm of a cell takes up most of the cell's space. It's a substance that is like jelly, and is made of chemicals and water. The nucleus is in the middle of the cell, separate from the cytoplasm. DNA is inside this tiny nucleus.

Imagine taking a ladder, holding it still at the top and bottom, and then twisting the ladder. This is what DNA looks like. Ladders have rungs, or steps that you can walk up. DNA has structures that look like rungs. They are called base pairs, which are made of four different kinds of building blocks. These building blocks can only be paired in certain ways. If they are not matched correctly, the cell may die.

Compared to other parts of the cell, DNA molecules are very long. How do they fit? They coil and twist inside the nucleus. What does DNA do? DNA carries the information for physical traits.

Identical twins develop from an egg and sperm that split just a few days after the baby is conceived. The baby's traits have already been planned by DNA. Splitting the cell means the same traits are in each half of the split. That's why identical twins are always the same sex. Identical twins don't always grow up exactly the same, though. As they grow, they are affected by their environment. Even twins who are separated may have similar personalities and degrees of intelligence. Some twins who find each other after years of living apart are amazed at how similar they are!

Some physical traits are linked to proteins. That means that the DNA has the instructions to make proteins. Proteins have many jobs. An enzyme is a protein that makes a chemical reaction in your body, like digesting your food. Another kind of protein, called a transport protein, carries important substances in your body. Other kinds of proteins protect you from diseases or build your blood.

Each set of identical twins share common traits, such as the shape of their facial features.

DNA is only part of the equation that makes you who you are. DNA molecules are found in genes, which are the basic units of heredity. Genes, in turn, are located on structures called **chromosomes**, which come in pairs. Humans have twenty-three pairs of chromosomes, or forty-six chromosomes in all. One chromosome in each pair comes from your mother. The other comes from your father. Unless you are an identical twin, no one has the same genetic information as you.

Chromosomes even decide if you are a boy or a girl. The chromosomes that decide if you are a male or female are called sex chromosomes. They can be either X or Y. Females always have two X chromosomes. Males have one X and one Y chromosome. The mother always gives an X chromosome to the child, while the father may give an X or a Y. So the father is the parent who determines whether a child is a boy or a girl.

Look at these traits! They were determined by genes.

Free Earlobe
A free earlobe hangs below the point where it's attached to your head.

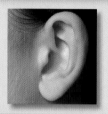

Attached Earlobe
An attached ear lobe is attached to the side of your head.

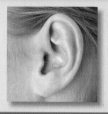

Dimples
Dimples look like indentations on the right or left side of your mouth.

No Dimples
If you have no dimples, your face looks smooth when you smile.

Straight Pinky
Straight pinkies point straight up.

Bent Pinky
More people have bent pinkies than straight ones.

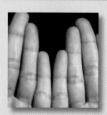

Tongue-Rolling
More people can roll up their tongues than cannot do so.

Not Rolling
If you have this trait, you can't roll up the sides of your tongue!

What happens if the chromosomes don't pair up the right way? Human cells normally contain twenty-three pairs of chromosomes. If the number changes, all sorts of problems can happen with the growth, development, and functioning of body systems. Some problems with chromosomes occur even before the mother and father's cells combine to create a baby. Other problems can occur while the mother is pregnant. There are different problems with chromosomes. Down Syndrome, for example, is caused when three chromosomes are all in a space where there should only be two. That means someone with Down Syndrome has forty-seven chromosomes in each cell instead of forty-six. While science often helps doctors detect problems with chromosomes, we still don't always know how to prevent problems, or how to solve them.

Stretch your arm in front of you, make a fist, and turn it with your thumb pointing up. Then give the thumbs up sign. Take a look! Is your thumb straight, or is it curved? A curved or straight thumb is a genetic trait. Take a look at the chart on page 8 for other inherited traits. Which do you have? Ask your family members if their traits are the same! Do you see any trends in your family?

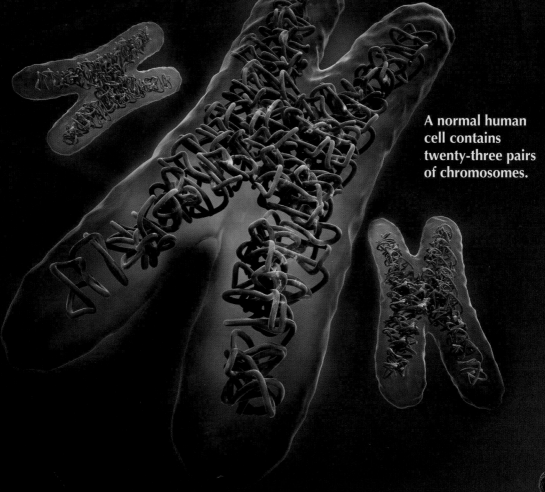

A normal human cell contains twenty-three pairs of chromosomes.

Early Ideas About Genetics

People have asked questions about heredity for a long time. Ancient people observed that cows only gave birth to cows. They knew if they planted wheat seeds, only wheat would grow. What did people long ago know about genetics?

Because of genetics, an elephant gives birth to another elephant. Babies look like miniature versions of their parents.

Ancient people had their own ideas about genetics and heredity.

A Greek philosopher named Theophrastus had a **theory** about why flowers bloomed. He thought there were male flowers and female flowers. The male flowers would make female flowers ripen. But it's not quite that simple.

A Greek doctor, Hippocrates, wanted to explain why babies had traits of both their mothers and fathers. Hippocrates thought about plant seeds. He decided that babies grow from seeds. At the time a baby was created, seeds from both the mother's body and the father's body would combine to make one seed to help a baby grow.

Another thinker in ancient Greece, Pythagoras, thought that only the male was really a parent. All the baby's traits came from the father. The mother was there just to carry the baby until it was born.

Have you ever heard of a family being described as blood relatives? Have you ever heard the word *bloodline* used to explain the relationship between people in a family? Those words may have come from the ideas of a man in ancient Greece. His name was Aristotle. He believed that both parents contributed to the traits of an unborn baby. He also believed the traits came from the mother and father's blood. People believed these ideas for almost two thousand years.

Another thinker, Empedocles, thought that parts of both the mother and father combined to make a baby. This idea is much closer to science as we know it today.

550 B.C.E.	Pythagoras states that the male parent is the only parent who passes on traits to the offspring.
453 B.C.E.	Empedocles says that both male and female material comes together to create new life.
1637	Jan Swammerdam is born. He later proposes that each sperm contains the entire human being.
1720	Charles Bonnet is born. He proposes that each egg contains the entire human being.
1733	Kaspar Friedrich Wolff is born. He states that the egg and sperm both contain particles that combine traits.

People's ideas about genetics stayed the same for a long time. Scientists needed new tools to study them. The Renaissance (from about the fourteenth to the sixteenth centuries) was a time of deep thinking about science and art. Scientists of that era were limited, though. Why were they limited? For example, they didn't have microscopes! Without microscopes, they didn't know about cells and parts of cells. Let's look at a few more ideas about heredity and genetics.

The creation of a baby requires both an egg from a mother and sperm from a father. Scientists figured this out, but they still did not understand how each part combined to create a baby with traits from both parents. Scientists had opposing views of how the egg and sperm combined. Some believed that the sperm contained an entire human being. It would grow inside the mother. Others believed that a complete human being was contained in the egg. That means people would be linked only to their mother.

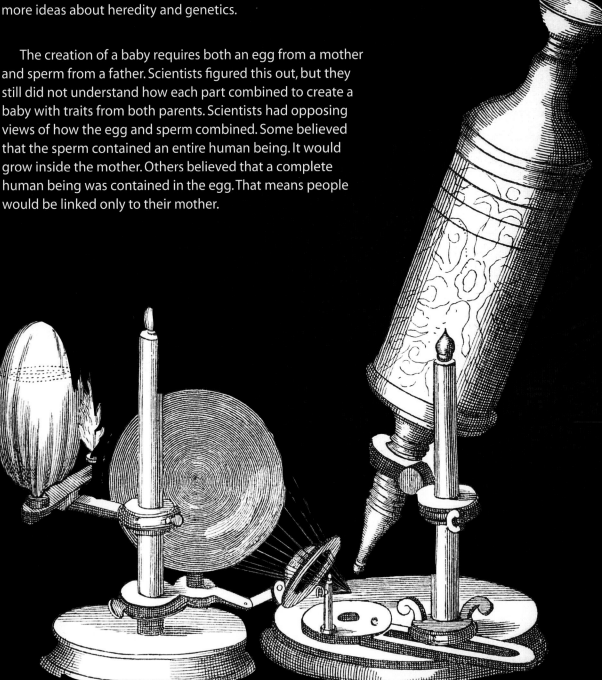

Early microscopes like Robert Hooke's first allowed scientists to study cells.

Microscopes sure have changed over the years! Now we can get a clearer view of cells—and their tiny parts.

In the seventeenth century, Robert Hooke was a busy scientist! He studied physics, astronomy, biology, chemistry, and even architecture. Hooke had many accomplishments. He created a spring that made accurate clocks possible. He invented an early model of a respirator. He even helped rebuild London after a huge fire burned down much of the city. In the field of genetics his invention of the microscope changed the course of science. Hooke could use it to observe cells. The first cells he examined were taken from thin slices of cork. His invention paved the way for so many more observations about the natural world.

Finally, the microscope was invented. Scientists could see cells. They still struggled to figure out how traits were passed down in families. One biologist, by the name of August Weismann, experimented with mice at the end of the nineteenth century. In twenty-two generations of mice, he cut off the tails of the parents. He thought that this trait would be passed on to baby mice. Of course, all the baby mice were born with tails. Scientists started thinking: What traits can be passed on? What traits cannot be passed on?

Darwin and Evolution

How old is Earth? Scientists estimate that Earth is 4.5 billion years old. Life-forms here have evolved during that time. We've come a long way! In the early 1800s, most scientists thought Earth was only six thousand years old.

What's so important about Earth's age? Let's compare what we know now to what people thought two hundred years ago. We know today that evolution takes a long time. If Earth were only six thousand years old, there wouldn't have been enough time for species to have evolved. The same people who thought Earth was six thousand years old believed that people ruled animals. Naturalists in the early 1800s didn't want to believe that people were in the same family as cows or birds. Charles Darwin challenged these beliefs and helped us learn more about life on Earth.

As a child, Darwin was very happy reading or collecting shells and beetles outside. As he grew, he developed a love for science, but his dad wanted him to be a doctor or minister. When he was in college, he struggled with his classes.

Darwin waited a long time to share his amazing ideas about heredity.

When he was supposed to be studying medicine, he was writing papers about things he noticed in nature. Then he got an invitation that changed his life!

Charles Darwin was only twenty-two years old when he took off on the voyage of a lifetime. He joined the crew of a ship, the HMS *Beagle*. He was the **naturalist** on the ship. His job was to look at rocks, plants, and animals on and off the coast of South America. He filled dozens of notebooks with his careful observations. He collected rocks and bugs and other interesting natural things and sent them back to England. While he was observing and collecting, he started forming ideas that were remarkable. He decided that all animals were related. He realized that animals adapted to survive in their environments. He understood that the Earth had changed over a long period of time.

Have you ever seen a picture of a cactus at the South Pole? How about tall trees on the prairie? Why not? Plants have adaptations that help them live and grow in certain places. A desert has little rainfall. Plants there have different ways to survive. Some plants store water in stems or leaves. Others have long roots that spread far out from the plant to gather water. On the tundra, it's cold. There is little rain. Some of the plants there have dark leaves, which help them absorb what little heat they can get from the Sun.

Plants on the tundra can survive cold, dry conditions. The flowers move throughout the day toward the Sun.

Darwin noticed clues about the changing earth. He was in Chile when an earthquake struck. He noticed that a rocky ledge covered with shellfish, which used to be under the sea, was now above sea level. The earthquake had shifted the land 8 feet (about 2 meters) up! If an earthquake could do that, then, over millions of years, mountains could rise out of earth. Darwin's ideas started making people think. Was Earth older than six thousand years?

What did Darwin find that relates to genetics? Darwin didn't look just at geology. He also observed plants and animals. Off the coast of South America is a chain of islands called the Galápagos Islands. Darwin noticed many strange plants and animals there. They were different on the islands than on the mainland. How did they get there? Why were they so different?

Darwin was particularly fascinated by the giant tortoises that lived on the Galápagos Islands. He found that the tortoises were not the same on every island! Tortoises that lived on Hood Island had long necks, and shells that tipped up in front. These traits helped the tortoises eat tall plants, such as cactus. Tortoises that lived on Isabella Island had short necks and dome-shaped shells. These characteristics helped them eat plants that grew lower to the ground.

Darwin noticed that the shapes of the tortoises' shells and necks helped them eat the types of plants that grew on each island.

The diagram shows that many species came from the same original group.

The more plants and animals that Darwin saw, the more he realized that the plants and animals that survive are the ones that can adapt to their environment. Any animal that had some kind of advantage over the others could live longer. The advantages might include better-shaped beaks, the ability to live in a cold climate, color that helped the animal blend into its surroundings, or shells that provided protection. These traits were passed on to the organism's offspring in each generation.

Even before Darwin published his findings, people debated the ideas. Fifty years before Darwin's book, William Paley wrote a book. He said living things were complex. They could only be made by an intelligent creator. In 1925 there was a famous trial in the United States about evolution. A biology teacher named John Scopes taught evolution in his class. He was arrested for teaching that people evolved from animals. In some schools today students learn about both evolution and intelligent design.

Mendel and Genetics

He's called the "Father of Genetics" for his work. He was a monk, not a famous scientist. He discovered important ideas about genetics from growing and observing simple pea plants. Who was he? He was Gregor Mendel.

The idea of breeding animals and plants to bring out their best traits has been around for thousands of years. Farmers knew that the strongest plants would come from the seeds of the very best plants. Their work wasn't very precise. They didn't know about heredity or genetics, so they just used trial and error.

Once the microscope had been invented, scientists were able to look at cells and see how they divided. They figured out more about how materials from parents combine to make offspring with shared traits. Scientists really didn't understand how it happened, though. Many scientists tried to unlock this mystery.

Gregor Mendel was not a well-known scientist. He was a teacher who did basic genetic research. His ideas were groundbreaking, but no one knew about them until long after Mendel died. Once he had conducted his experiments, he went on to live a quiet life as a monk.

This drawing shows Mendel studying his pea plants.

Apple growers use genetics to grow apples with the best traits.

Mendel did his research with pea plants over many generations of plants. He chose pea plants because they have traits that are easy to observe. These include flower color, flower position, length of stem, seed shape, seed color, pod shape, and pod color. They are also easy to grow, and they grow quickly. Mendel wanted to trace the traits through several generations.

When you think about the pea plant traits, you can compare them to human traits. Imagine that two parents have the same eye color. Yet, their child has eyes of a different color. Most of the scientists who lived during Darwin's time thought that traits like eye color came from the parents and were passed on to the children. Yet, children can have the same color eyes as their grandparents. What can explain that mystery?

You may have heard about hybrid cars. Have you heard of a hybrid animal or plant? A hybrid animal has parents of two different species. They are pretty close together, like a horse and zebra. The name of the hybrid animal has the names of both parents, with the father's name first. A liger is the baby of a male lion and female tiger. What if mom were a lion and dad a tiger? You'd have a tigon! Some hybrid animals cannot have babies. We use many hybrid plants. Most wheat plants, for example, are hybrids. Seedless watermelons are hybrids, too!

A mule is the offspring of a donkey and a horse.

Mendel pondered the idea that traits move from one generation to the next. He also thought about an idea from Charles Darwin. Darwin believed that our bodies had heredity particles. The particles could change based on the environment surrounding us. This idea wasn't really right either. Mendel set out to test these ideas.

Mendel **cross-pollinated** different kinds of pea plants. He started by cross-pollinating pea plants that have yellow seeds and pea plants that have green seeds. All of the plants that resulted from that combination had yellow seeds. Mendel then cross-pollinated those plants. In the next generation, most of the plants had yellow seeds. As he grew more generations of plants, Mendel discovered that three times as many plants had yellow seeds as had green seeds. This happened in every generation of pea plants.

What did Mendel find out from these simple plants and their seeds? He found out that some genes are **dominant**. This means they are more likely to occur. In pea plants, yellow seeds are dominant, even when yellow-seeded and green-seeded plants are combined. Other genes are **recessive**. They are less likely to occur.

Mendel discovered important ideas that became the foundation for genetics. He learned that basic heredity traits do not combine. The pea plants with yellow and green seeds did not make plants with seeds that were yellowish-green. Instead, traits are passed along intact. Some of the plants had green seeds; some had yellow. Mendel learned that each parent gives half of its traits to offspring. Some traits are more dominant than others. Not every offspring inherits traits the same way. That's why two siblings might share some traits but don't look exactly alike.

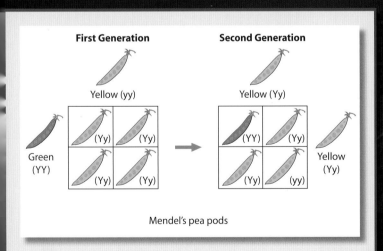

First Generation

Yellow (yy)

Green (YY)

(Yy) (Yy)
(Yy) (Yy)

Second Generation

Yellow (Yy)

Yellow (Yy)

(YY) (Yy)
(Yy) (yy)

Mendel's pea pods

A plant with green seeds and a plant with yellow seeds produced only plants with yellow seeds. In the next generation, three out of four plants had yellow seeds.

Have you ever seen a peacock like this? It has no pigment, so all its feathers are white.

Many creatures, like polar bears, are naturally white. Some white animals may have a condition called albinism. A recessive gene causes albinism. When the offspring gets this recessive gene from both parents, the organism cannot make the right amount of pigment, which gives skin, fur, or feathers their colors. An albino alligator, for example, is completely white instead of green or brown. This causes a real problem for wild animals. An all-white animal is much easier for a predator to spot. People with albinism can protect themselves by wearing sunglasses, sunscreen, and protective clothing.

Jumping genes are responsible for the changing colors in each ear of corn.

What Are Jumping Genes?

Gregor Mendel showed that a pea plant with yellow seeds and a pea plant with green seeds combine to make a plant with yellow seeds or green seeds. The colors didn't mix. Some ears of corn, though, break this rule!

Have you ever seen an ear of Indian corn? The grains on a cob of Indian corn are all different colors, like purple, yellow, red, or white. Yet, if you look closely, you might see kernels with multiple colors. A white grain, for example, could have red streaks on it. This goes exactly against Mendel's studies. Mendel's laws would predict that the corn kernels should be solid colors.

Dr. Barbara McClintock, one of the few women to win a Nobel Prize in science, was fascinated with studying corn. In 1957 she started research on corn, or maize, in South America. She and groups of scientists studied maize in South America for over twenty years! Her work on the genetics of corn solved the mystery of the multicolored corn kernels.

McClintock isolated a gene called a transposon, which is a gene that moves from one location to another on a chromosome. Imagine a chromosome layer that has pigment, or color, on it. Now a transposon jumps onto the gene and sits on top of one of the genes that makes pigments. With the transposon there, the gene is blocked.

Transposons have an unkind name. Scientists call them selfish DNA. Why? It seems like their only real function is to copy themselves. They are also called junk DNA, because they have no benefit to their **hosts**. But, if we look more closely, we can find instances in which transposons help organisms. People have developed chemicals to get rid of pests like fruit flies. Transposons in the genes of fruit flies have been linked to **resistance**. The fruit flies are more resistant to the chemicals. Maybe we don't think the transposons are good in this case. Fruit flies are probably grateful, though!

McClintock's work with corn led to important discoveries about far more than corn!

That means the color is blocked. So a grain that would have been red is now red with white streaks. If the transposon jumps again, there's another white streak. This goes on all over the corn cob in multiple grains of corn as the transposons jump from gene to gene. The results may vary, though. If the transposon stays in one place long enough, the whole grain could turn white. Or the grains of corn could be streaked, blotched, or dotted.

Scientists search for new ways to boost people's health.

Transposons definitely make Indian corn look pretty, but why was their discovery so important? After all, McClintock spent years and years working with the maize and won an award for her work. It must have been special.

McClintock's discovery goes much further than corn! In recent years, for example, scientists have found a clear link between jumping genes and **immunity**. Our immune systems are able to react when different substances attack them. A jumping gene can create major changes in DNA, some that can even change future generations of organisms. Some of the changes are not so good. Some researchers believe that transposons are responsible for causing some kinds of cancers and other diseases. Yet, transposons can be helpful as well. A transposon that scientists call Hermes (named after a messenger in mythology) moves quickly in genes to look for antigens, which are substances that fight diseases in the body. This transposon figures out which proteins are safe in the body and which could make the body sick. The transposon builds antibodies to fight the infection. This discovery is exciting for scientists. By studying the transposons, scientists might be able to figure out how the body fights infection and disease.

Scientists are also using transposons to move genetic material from one gene to another. They have discovered a way to create transposons in a lab. Scientists sometimes use **viruses** to move genetic material throughout the body, but viruses do not always behave in a predictable way. The synthetic, or manufactured, transposons are safer than viruses.

A gene map shows patterns of chromosomes in a particular living organism. Genetic maps help scientists and doctors better understand genes. Understanding the patterns of genes can help show how species are linked to other species.

The Human **Genome** Project was huge! Scientists spent thirteen years identifying the genes in human DNA, 25,000 in all. Then they determined the sequence of 3 billion base pairs that make human DNA. The U.S. government led this project with countries all over the world. Why did scientists take on this huge project? For many reasons! Learning more about genes can help doctors diagnose, prevent, and treat diseases. Genetic information can help scientists create new sources of energy and find better ways to solve crimes.

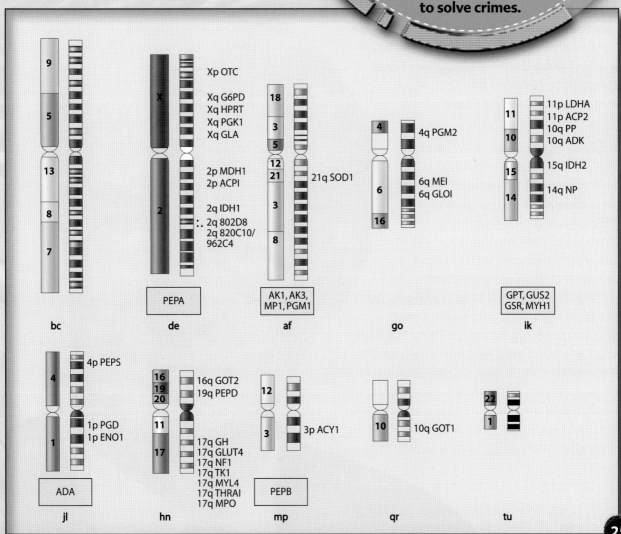

Linus Pauling and the Race for DNA

Linus Pauling was a scientist, author, peace activist, and teacher. He informed people about the dangers of nuclear war, warned people about the hazards of smoking, and educated people about the benefits of vitamins. He was also fascinated by DNA!

Linus Pauling had many interests, including DNA.

Linus Pauling was one of many people who had the same goal. They all wanted to figure out the structure of DNA. DNA is arranged in a double helix, or double spiral, with all the base pairs lined up along the spirals. There was fierce competition between scientists who all wanted to discover this shape.

James Watson was a biologist in Indiana who worked with Francis Crick, a physicist in England. Their work together began to confirm their earliest beliefs, that the structure of DNA was indeed a helix. Other scientists were working toward the same goal. Linus Pauling had already discovered the helix structure of a protein. He thought that DNA must be arranged the same way. Rosalind Franklin was a young chemist working in Paris on DNA. Another chemist, Erwin Chargaff, examined DNA's structure, too. He was the first person who identified all the substances in base pairs. Many talented people, one goal: to prove without a doubt the shape of DNA. The race was on!

Watson and Crick started building models. They used balls and sticks to try to make the DNA structure. Their first idea was a triple helix. The pairs were all pointed outward from the model. Watson and Crick knew their idea wouldn't work. They kept plugging away.

While they were working, Pauling created a model of his own. He was going to travel to England to a conference to see some data about DNA that Franklin had found with X rays, but the U.S. government would not let him leave the country. So, Pauling's son went to England to discuss his father's DNA model. Watson and Crick figured they had a lead on Pauling. They could prove the structure first!

Sickle cell anemia is a disease linked to genes. What exactly is it? A normal red blood cell is round. It flows easily through your veins, bringing a protein called hemoglobin to your body. Hemoglobin brings oxygen. A sickle cell isn't round—it's shaped like a C. These cells have a harder time traveling through veins, so the body doesn't get enough oxygen. Sickle cells don't live very long, either. The body has a hard time making enough cells to prevent pain and tiredness. To get sickle cell anemia, you have to have a sickle cell gene passed down from each parent.

The C-shaped cell is a sickle cell.

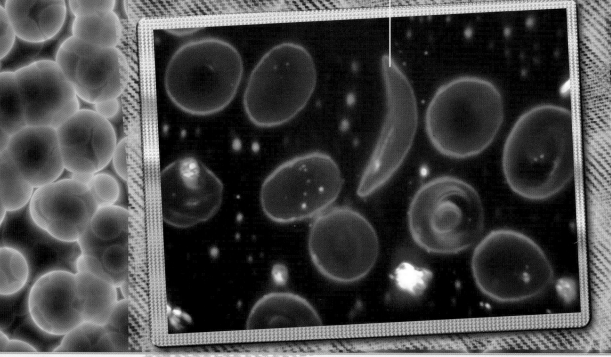

The story of the race has twists and turns. Franklin had a photo of DNA material that she had created from X rays. Watson and Crick sketched a copy of the photo and modeled the structure of DNA. Watson and Crick published a paper about the discovery. Franklin didn't publish or share her photograph, even though she had discussed it with other scientists. Sadly, Franklin died from cancer at a young age, most likely because of the X rays with which she worked. Crick and Watson shared the Nobel Prize for the discovery, along with Maurice Wilkins, a scientist who had worked on developing the atomic bomb.

What about Linus Pauling? He didn't get credit for discovering the double helix. Yet, he still was extremely interested in science and made many valuable contributions. Before Pauling worked with plasma DNA modeling, he was the first to understand the cause of sickle cell anemia.

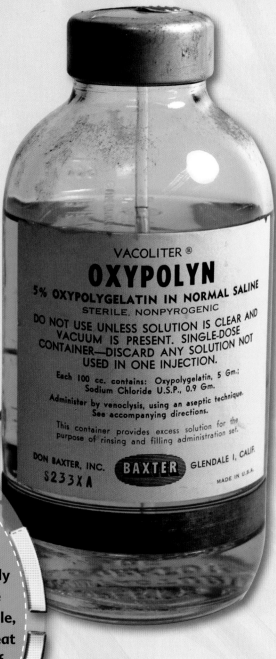

Many chemical reactions happen in your body all the time. Your body has everything it needs to make some reactions happen. For some reactions your body needs a vitamin to get it going. Your body doesn't make vitamins. Where do they come from? The foods you eat! Vitamin A, for example, is important to your eyes and skin. When you eat foods like carrots, your stomach turns part of the carrots into vitamin A. Vitamin D helps your bones grow. You can get vitamin D by drinking milk, eating eggs, and by exposing yourself to sunlight!

Linus Pauling created a substance that could take the place of blood plasma.

Pauling researched for three years to discover that sickle cell anemia is caused by a defect in part of the blood. That defect was caused by two abnormal genes. Once Pauling identified the cause of sickle cell anemia, doctors began to think more about diseases. What other diseases were caused by abnormal genes?

During World War II Pauling used what he knew about protein and blood to craft a synthetic blood **plasma**. The plasma could easily be taken to battlefields and given to soldiers who had lost a lot of blood. Pauling invented devices, too. He created a meter to monitor the levels of oxygen in submarines and airplanes. After the war, his meter saved lives. Hospitals used it to monitor gas levels in incubators. The meter measured anesthesia levels during surgery.

Vitamins from A to E

There are many vitamins, but what do they do? This chart shows a few vitamins that are important to your health and growth.

Vitamin	What does it do?	Where can you find it?
A	helps eyesight and growth	liver, carrots, egg yolks, green leafy vegetables
B1	makes strong muscles and a healthy digestive system	liver, rice, yeast, peanuts
B2	creates healthy skin, nails, and hair; helps digestion	milk, yeast, cheese, fish, green leafy vegetables
C	protects from viruses and bacteria; heals wounds; prevents diseases	citrus fruits, berries, tomatoes, cauliflower, potatoes, peppers
D	creates strong bones and teeth	sunlight, cod-liver oil, sardines, salmon, tuna, milk
E	fights toxins in your body	nuts, soy beans, vegetable oil, broccoli, sprouts

Genetics and Medicine

You know that genes are responsible for your eye color, your height, and the way your earlobes hang! Genes, unfortunately, can also cause diseases. Doctors are figuring out new ways to detect and treat genetic diseases.

Think about the numbers that go with genes! There are forty-six human chromosomes. In those chromosomes, there are almost 3 billion base pairs of DNA. The DNA has between 30,000 and 40,000 genes that make protein. A disease or disorder can happen when just one gene has a **mutation**. One of the biggest problems facing doctors and scientists is figuring out how genes contribute to the inheritance of a disease. In some diseases, like asthma, there isn't just one disease gene. There might be mutations in several genes. There might be things in the environment that react with genes to cause disease. Some of the mysteries of genes and disease have been unraveled. Yet, many more remain. We'll look at just a few diseases that are related to genes.

Cancer is a mutation of cells. Sometimes, environmental factors cause cancer. Smoking tobacco, for example, is an environmental factor that can contribute to lung cancer. Genes are often part of cancer, as well. Some cancers, like breast cancer, have clear genetic links. Researchers have identified some cell mutations that would signal someone is at greater risk for breast cancer. Leukemia is a cancer in blood cells. Doctors can diagnose leukemia by looking for an abnormal chromosome.

A cancer cell is a cell that has mutated. It looks and behaves differently from healthy cells.

This is a healthy cell. It looks different from a cancer cell.

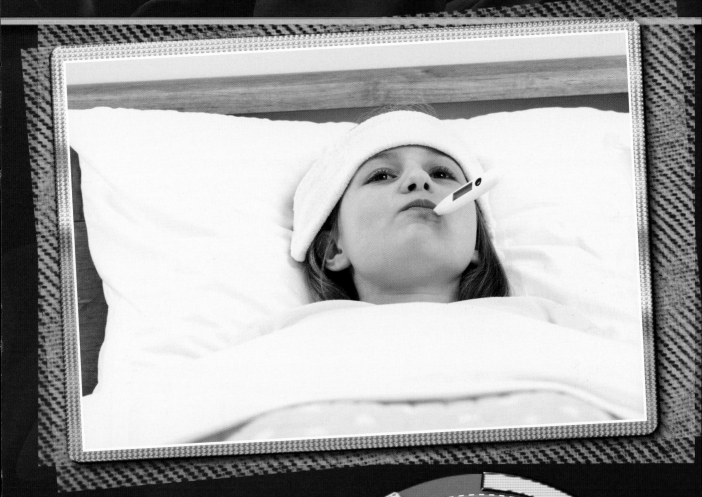

Do you get a lot of colds? You might have a weak immune system.

Type 1 diabetes is a disease that makes it hard for the body to convert food into energy. Someone with Type 1 diabetes is more likely to have blindness, heart disease, and kidney failure. Is Type 1 diabetes genetic? Doctors call Type 1 diabetes a complex trait. In simpler language this means that it takes mutations in several genes to cause the disease. Researchers have pinpointed which chromosome is most likely to **mutate**. Even though doctors can pinpoint this chromosome, they don't know how to use this information to prevent Type 1 diabetes.

Parasites, microbes, bacteria—they're attacking your body! What protects you? Skin helps, but that's part of a larger system: your immune system. The skin is a barrier against things invading your body. Germs can get in through openings: your mouth, nose, and eyes. Your tears break down germs. Cells lining your nose, mouth, and throat repel bacteria, too. Anything that gets through has to deal with your blood cells, bone marrow, your spleen, and more. What does this have to do with genetics? Genetics can determine your immune system's strength. Your immune system can fight off some genetic disorders, too.

Pinpointing genetic diseases is a step toward better health. Treatments for these diseases have become better over the years. Doctors are looking at new approaches—called gene therapy—to treating these diseases, too.

Gene therapy might be able to correct faulty genes. Doctors can take a gene that doesn't work and replace it with a normal gene. An abnormal gene may be able to be reversed. If it were damaged, a repair could take it back to its normal state. Doctors can also regulate a gene, which is a lot like turning the gene on or off. The most common method is to replace an abnormal gene with a normal one. But genes are tiny! A doctor can't just take a needle, pull out a gene, and put a new gene in. The new genes need to be attached to something that can travel through the body. Viruses can move quickly. Doctors have figured out a way to attach normal genes to viruses. They can send these viruses racing through the body to the infected areas.

A doctor asks questions to figure out your genetic history.

DNA-Based Gene Tests

There are more than one thousand genetic tests available today. This chart shows just a few of the many diseases that may be detected with a gene test.

Disease	Symptoms
Amyotrophic Lateral Sclerosis (ALS): Lou Gehrig's Disease	Slowing down of motor functions, which eventually leads to paralysis and death
Gaucher Disease	Enlarged liver and spleen; bone loss
Central Core Disease	Weakness of muscles
Cystic Fibrosis	Chronic infections
Fragile X Syndrome	Leading cause of mental retardation
Hemophilia	Bruising and uncontrollable bleeding
Spinal Muscular Atrophy	Muscle weakness
Tay-Sachs Disease	Seizures; paralysis

Gene therapy has not been very successful so far. When normal cells are placed into the body, they do what other cells do. They rapidly divide. When the cells divide, they don't do as good a job at fighting the disease. So gene therapy has to be repeated. Another problem with gene therapy is our body's immune system. Our bodies attack anything coming in that shouldn't be there. The immune system might prevent the new cells from entering the body. Finally, many of the diseases that doctors would most like to treat are caused by problems with more than one gene. Pinpointing a way to get normal cells to all these genes is almost impossible!

A genetic family tree shows the ages and causes of relatives' deaths. The tree plots out who in a family inherited a disease—and who did not. Why would you go to genetic counseling? If a family member has a health problem like diabetes or high blood pressure, your doctor can help prevent or treat it. If parents have a baby with a genetic disease, they might want to find out how likely it is that their next baby would have the same problem. Genetic counseling doesn't always prevent problems, but it can help people be prepared to treat them.

Solving Crimes with Genetics

You're watching an old detective movie. The detective sprinkles powder on a surface. Then he takes a brush, dusts the surface, and presses a piece of paper to the powder. How has crime-solving changed because of genetics?

Forensic scientists use chemistry to solve crimes!

Forensics is the science and technology that is used to investigate facts in court cases. When detectives gather a hair sample, a piece of clothing, or a fingerprint, they are collecting forensic evidence. Evidence can show whether a person was at a crime scene and whether that person may have committed that crime.

It makes sense for detectives to use DNA to identify criminals. After all, unless you have an identical twin, no one shares your DNA.

The first time someone in the United States was convicted because of DNA was in 1987, so this science is still pretty new.

Fingerprints were important in ancient civilizations. In Babylon, businessmen sealed deals with fingerprints. In ancient China, clay seals had thumbprints. In 1686 Marcello Malpighi named parts of the fingerprint: ridges, spirals, and loops. About the same time, an Englishman, Sir William Herschel, asked someone to put his handprint on a contract. Herschel collected more fingerprints. He realized they were all different! In the past century, governments have used fingerprints to identify criminals. Why are fingerprints important to detectives? No two fingerprints have been found to be alike, even in billions of comparisons made by computers.

Fingerprint analysis has been used for over one hundred years! Now forensics experts can create DNA fingerprints. It's simple to make a fingerprint. You put your finger on a stamp pad and press down on paper. A DNA fingerprint is much more complicated. First, the investigator has to collect DNA, which can come from a hair, a drop of blood, saliva, or from a personal item like a toothbrush. Investigators collect DNA from four or five places at a crime scene and also from the suspected criminal. Once the DNA is collected, it's analyzed to create a DNA profile. The profiles are compared. Are the profiles at the scene different from the suspect's profile? That means that the suspect most likely was not at the scene. But if the profiles match, then that suspect may have committed the crime. Some experts aren't sure how many matches must happen before they can consider the evidence solid. This method, though, is much better than relying on people who may have seen the crime. Statistics show those eyewitnesses are only right half the time.

Fingerprints are still important evidence in crime investigation since no two fingerprints are alike.

Forensic DNA is used for many things other than proving innocence or guilt. One project that uses DNA is called the DNA Shoah Project. This project is a database with genetic profiles of families who lost family members during the Holocaust. The genetic profiles can bring lost family members together. When unidentified bodies are uncovered in graves, their DNA may be matched in the database so that the victims can be identified.

In the 1990s a family discovered that one of its family members, Michael Blassie, had been buried in the Tomb of the Unknown Soldier. The Tomb of the Unknown Soldier is a tomb in Arlington National Ceremony in which the remains of unidentified soldiers have been placed.

Michael Blassie's family knew that he had died in the Vietnam War, but they had never recovered his body. He died in 1972, and his body—still unidentified—was placed in the tomb in 1984. Ten years later, Blassie's family members thought that he might be buried in the tomb. They asked government officials to test the body. DNA testing matched Blassie to his family. His body was removed from the tomb so that his family could bury him closer to home.

A football used during the Super Bowl is a prize for a collector. If someone tried to sell you an authentic Super Bowl football, how would you know it was the real thing? For the 2008 Super Bowl a company marked each football used in the game with a strand of synthetic DNA. You can only see the DNA if the football is lit by a laser. DNA is used in other unique ways. DNA is being collected from endangered animals. The DNA helps scientists identify animals and could someday help save entire species.

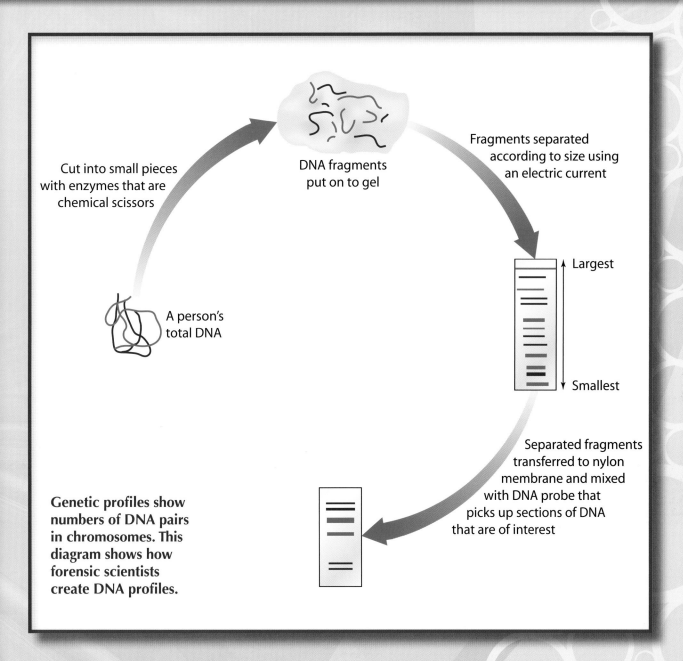

Cut into small pieces
with enzymes that are
chemical scissors

DNA fragments
put on to gel

Fragments separated
according to size using
an electric current

A person's
total DNA

Largest

Smallest

Separated fragments
transferred to nylon
membrane and mixed
with DNA probe that
picks up sections of DNA
that are of interest

**Genetic profiles show
numbers of DNA pairs
in chromosomes. This
diagram shows how
forensic scientists
create DNA profiles.**

Not everyone believes that DNA testing is the best way to convict criminals. DNA samples can reveal a lot about a person, like what diseases that person has. A fingerprint just identifies a criminal, but a DNA profile might tell things that other people shouldn't be allowed to know, such as whether they are prone to certain illnesses.

It's hard to sample and store DNA, but in some states, it is stored for a long time. This means that people may be able to find out private information about people who were arrested, even if they were never convicted of crimes.

Genetic Engineering
The Future of Food?

Roses with longer-lasting flowers, corn plants with more ears of corn, and soybeans that grow in dry soil. What do these things have in common? Some of them might be genetically engineered!

For centuries, people have created better plants and animals by doing something called selective breeding. This means that if you wanted better corn plants, you'd take the best corn from your field and use the seeds from only those plants to make new plants. If you needed a good hunting dog, you would find the best female hunting dog and the best male hunting dog so that their offspring might be even better at hunting. These processes are natural. Farmers who bred their plants and animals did not use DNA. They chose the best parents to create new offspring. It might take years for the best hunting dog or the best corn to develop, but being patient could bring great results.

What if you wanted the process to move along more quickly? Genetic engineering can be used to speed things up. Scientists simply take the genes from one plant and insert them into the cells of another to combine the best traits of both. What are some of the benefits of this kind of bioengineered food?

By thinking deliberately about which genes should go into a plant, scientists can make food that is more nutritious and better tasting. In areas with little water a plant could be created that needs less water. A plant like this would be more likely to live. If pests are problems to a crop, farmers have usually used some kind of **pesticide** to get rid of them. But a genetically engineered plant might get rid of the need for pesticides. That would make crops safer to eat and help the environment around the crops. Plants can grow faster, and products can have a longer shelf life. Scientists are even working on edible vaccines. Instead of getting a shot, you could eat a potato! In some places, potatoes would be easier to ship and to store than vaccines.

Scientists add genes from one plant to another to make new plants with better traits.

Genetically engineered plants can grow in harsh conditions.

You are a farmer in a poor country. Your soil is dry. The weather is hot. Pests are in the fields. How can you grow rice? Scientists developed a great-tasting rice that grows under the worst conditions. How did they do it? One team took the gene that creates a simple sugar and introduced that gene to a certain kind of rice. The sugar, called trehalose, is not found in many plants. Instead, it's found in mushrooms and insects. When the sugar was added to the rice plant, it resisted dry conditions. It could even be watered with salt water!

When you go to the store, are you picking up genetically engineered foods off the shelf? Actually, you probably aren't eating too many whole fruits and vegetables that have been genetically modified. Many of these products are not available in supermarkets, because scientists are figuring out the best ways to test them for safety. They want to make sure that people won't be allergic to genetically engineered foods. If you were allergic to peanuts, for example, you could be allergic to any food that has DNA added from peanuts.

Genetically engineered foods are more likely to be ingredients in other products you eat. Soybeans are one of the biggest genetically engineered crops in the United States and around the world. You don't usually eat soybeans by themselves, but they show up in other foods, such as cereal and cooking oils. That means your breakfast this morning could have been genetically engineered. Cotton is a major crop that is genetically engineered. You could be wearing a genetically engineered t-shirt!

Not all tomatoes are genetically engineered! However, many of these foods have genetically engineered versions.

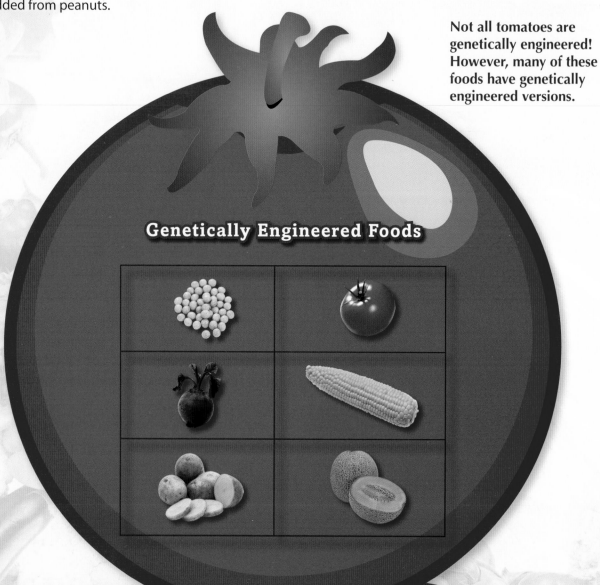

Genetically Engineered Foods

When you eat breakfast cereal with genetically engineered soybeans as an ingredient, you probably don't see a big label on the front that says "Made with genetically engineered soybeans." That's because people are still trying to figure out how they should label these products or whether they should label them at all. Although many consider these foods safe, some people still wonder. How much do people need to know about the foods they are eating? How can the labels give them accurate information? These are some of the questions that we need to answer as more of our foods are created, as well as grown.

Genetically engineered foods could be more nutritious, faster-growing, and maybe even tastier! So why would they be surrounded by controversy? One problem is that genetically engineered food is expensive to make. There are countries around the world where people are poor, and food is scarce. Engineering is too expensive to help people in many of these places. Some genetically engineered food made around the world isn't labeled. You could be eating engineered food without knowing it. Some people also wonder if we even need genetically engineered foods at all.

This hot dog might contain many genetically engineered foods, from lettuce to the wheat used to make the bun.

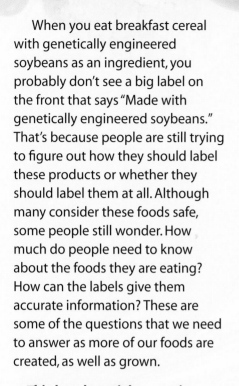

Genetics and the Future

Fifty years ago genetics was a relatively new science. Advances in genetics are being made almost every day! Where will genetics lead us in the future? Only time will tell!

We've learned about the fascinating history of genetics and ways we use genetic information today. When we think about these fields, new questions arise. We wonder about the choices we have to make because of genetics. We wonder what else we might unlock about this powerful science. We look forward to the lives that we can lead, made better by science!

Genetics and Medicine

Researchers are closing in on determining the role that genes play in disease. They continue to develop screening tests for diseases and hunt for cures. Tests that can screen for genetic diseases may not always cure diseases. People who undergo genetic screening, though, might find they are at risk for a disease and notice warning signs earlier. Questions continue to surround genetics and medicine. Some of the testing and treatments are expensive. Who decides who will get these tests and treatments? Some people aren't sure if the treatments are effective. All in all, it will take patience, time, and continued testing to bring genetics and medicine to a huge amount of patients.

Building Better Babies?

It sounds like science fiction. Take the DNA map of a genius. Duplicate that map in your unborn baby. Move around a few genes, and your baby is smarter than others. Move around a few more genes, and your baby is more athletic or better-looking. Believe it or not, some scientists think this kind of tinkering with genes is part of the future of genetics.

In the 1990s the number of jobs in genetics more than tripled. Many kinds of scientists work in genetics. Yet, many workers in genetics aren't scientists at all! Super computing and math skills are needed to track genetic information. Educators learn more to teach their students about genetics. A whole branch of law deals with questions related to DNA and genetics. Writers, graphic designers, and marketers can all work in the genetics field to advertise products, make biogenetic websites, and more. Genetic counseling is an entire field in medicine, with people looking to their DNA for answers to many questions.

These ideas scare many scientists. They fear that only the people who could afford the technology would have the option of creating "superhumans." If so, that would create an entirely different social class. It would take many studies of the long-term effects of manipulating genes to see if it were even safe!

The Isihara Test for Color Blindness

Most color blindness is genetic, although some people become color blind because of injuries. Color blindness makes it hard to see the differences between colors. The Isihara test determines whether a person can see different colors.

Can you see the number 12 in the circle? Some color-blind people cannot see it.

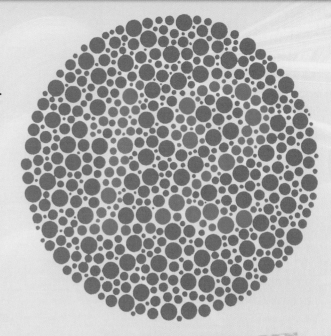

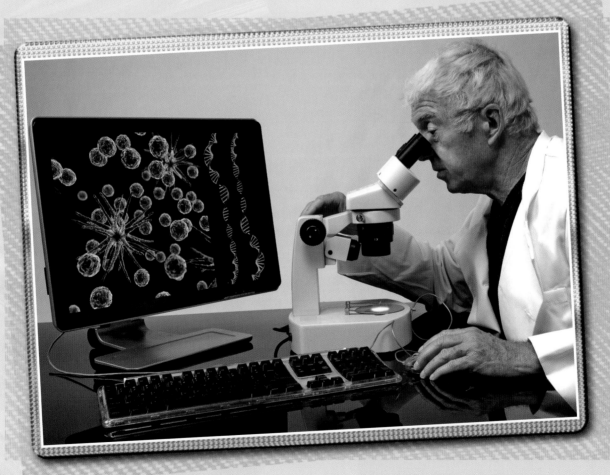

New technology provides new information about genetics.

Athletes and Genes

Athletes are expected to perform, and one of their main jobs is to keep their bodies strong and healthy. In the past, athletes have been caught and punished for using a type of drug called steroids. Steroids make them stronger but have very harmful side effects. What about gene therapy? After all, doctors can alter genes to make people healthier. Some athletes wonder, "Why not use genes to make me stronger and more able to compete?" In 2006 the U. S. Congress passed a law that banned gene doping in the United States. The law says that athletes are not allowed to use genes or genetic elements to make their performances better.

Is this good news? Most people think so. They believe that athletics is about talent and hard work, not drugs and science. After all, athletes probably inherited their talents. They were already born with athletic genes!

Cloning

What if you wanted to copy life? Twins look like copies; and in many ways, they are. Until very recently the idea of copying life seemed impossible. Cloning was an amazing scientific breakthrough. Scientists are trying to figure out the best uses for cloning.

Scientists use cloning and genetic alteration to make better plants. Will these techniques work on animals, too?

What if you had a beloved family pet and you wanted to make a copy of it before it died? What if you needed a liver transplant and a liver could be cloned inside another organism? We struggle with questions like these. Knowledge of genetics gives us great power. How do we use that power, and who benefits from it?

Charles Darwin's ideas were once considered unthinkable. Gregor Mendel used simple observations to open up a whole new way of thinking about how traits are passed on. Who knows what lies ahead in genetics? Whatever it is, it will be exciting to find out!

Dolly looked like any other white sheep. Dolly was special, though. She was the first cloned mammal. The team that created Dolly removed the nucleus from a sheep's cell. They inserted the nucleus into an unfertilized egg with its nucleus removed. The team tried this technique more than two hundred times. Dolly was the only sheep that lived. During her life, she gave birth to six lambs. Dolly lived for six years before she developed arthritis and a lung disease. Since Dolly's birth, other animals have been cloned, including horses, bulls, and dogs. Could cloning help save endangered species someday?

Dolly was the first cloned animal. She helped scientists understand the process and problems of cloning animals.

Glossary

chromosome A strand of DNA that carries genes.

cross-pollinate A process in which the pollen from one plant is delivered to the flower of another plant.

dominant A hereditary trait that is exhibited by the organism.

gene A substance that provides the instructions for cells.

genome A full set of chromosomes; all the inheritable traits of an organism.

host An animal or a plant that nourishes an organism without benefiting from it.

immunity The condition that permits either natural or acquired resistance to disease.

intelligent design The theory that everything in nature is the result of a single intelligence.

mutate Change from normal.

mutation A change in inherited characteristics, caused by a change in or damage to the DNA.

naturalist A person who studies natural history.

pesticide Chemicals used to kill insects.

plasma A pale liquid in blood that carries blood cells and platelets.

recessive A hereditary trait that does not exert itself.

resistance The ability to oppose or resist something.

theory An idea that explains a scientific event.

virus A microscopic agent that infects and replicates in living cells.

Find Out More

Books

Fridell, Ron. *Decoding Life: Unraveling Mysteries of the Genome.* Minneapolis, MN: Lerner Publications, 2004. This book, aimed at middle-school students, discusses DNA technologies and how they might change the world.

Perl, Lila. *Cloning.* New York: Marshall Cavendish, 2006. The controversial topics of genetically modifying crops, cloning animals, and patenting genes are discussed in this book.

Schacter, Bernice. *Genetics in the News.* New York: Chelsea House Publishers, 2007. This book gathers exciting news stories about topics in genetics, from the Human Genome Project and gene therapy to genetic engineering and the treatment of disease.

Spangenburg, Ray, and Kit Moser. *Genetic Engineering.* New York: Marshall Cavendish, 2004. Explores the Human Genome Project, the National Geographic Genographic Project, and stem-cell research.

Websites

www.amnh.org/ology/?channel=genetics&c
The American Museum of Natural History website offers online games, activities, interviews, and experiments related to genetic science.

www.dnaftb.org/dnaftb/
This website offers animated and illustrated explanations for the basic concepts of genetics, DNA, and chromosomes.

http://science.howstuffworks.com/genetic-science
This website offers multiple articles on genetic sciences, including forensic science, cloning, and genetic engineering.

Index